495

THE YOUNG FRENCH CHEF

Denise Perret * Mary Eckley

Illustrations by Catherine Cambier

Symbol of all French cooking, the wooden spoon is essential for the making of sauces, the glory of the French cuisine. It is the constant stirring of the sauce that assures its smoothness and the blending of delicate flavors. Use your wooden spoon well and it will produce for you the magic and mystery of the perfectly-cooked dish.

PLATT & MUNK

Publishers

New York

This book was awarded the Loisirs-Jeunes Prize for the best juvenile book published in France in 1965.
© Édicope 1965
Published in the United States by Platt & Munk in 1969. All rights reserved.
Manufactured in the United States of America. Library of Congress Catalog Card No. 70–75891

1

The Pleasure of Cooking

This book is intended as a beginning book of French cooking, to introduce American girls to the joys of French cuisine.

In cooking, you can express your own individuality and taste, perhaps more strongly than in any of the other arts. The kind of food you serve, the choice of menu, the seasoning and serving of the dishes, the dinner table itself, will all reflect your own personality. This is really the pleasure in cooking.

The French, with their traditional love for good food, give great care and attention to cooking even the simplest dish. Most of the recipes in this book are easy enough for the beginning cook. The desserts and some of the sauces are more difficult, but by the time you arrive at these, you should have made enough progress in your cooking skills to take them in stride.

French cooking, beloved of all gourmets, is unquestionably the most famous in all the world and is truly one of the fine arts. We hope this little collection of French recipes will inspire you to cook more often, to enjoy it, and in so doing, give yourself and your friends much pleasure.

BEFORE YOU BEGIN

Here are some things to remember before you begin to cook.

Put on an apron.

Wash your hands.

If you are roasting meat or deep-frying, protect your hair from odors with a scarf.

Close the door so the odors won't get into the rest of the house.

And, one thing more, be convinced that cooking is not work, but fun—because it is!

SOME WORDS OF CAUTION

Always use standard measures as described on Page 6.

Handle electric plugs with dry hands only.

Never light a gas oven until checking to see that the pilot light is on.

Be careful not to cut yourself when using a can opener.

Always turn the handle of a frying pan toward the wall, so that you won't accidentally knock it off the stove.

Never put cold water into frying oil; the oil will splatter.

Never fill a pot more than ¾ full; it may boil over.

Do not boil liquids too hard or the liquid will boil over.

When you're finished, turn off water and gas or electricity.

And, last but not least, always use good common sense in the kitchen.

TABLE OF CONTENTS

KITCHEN UTENSILS Les Ustensiles de Cuisine
(American Style)

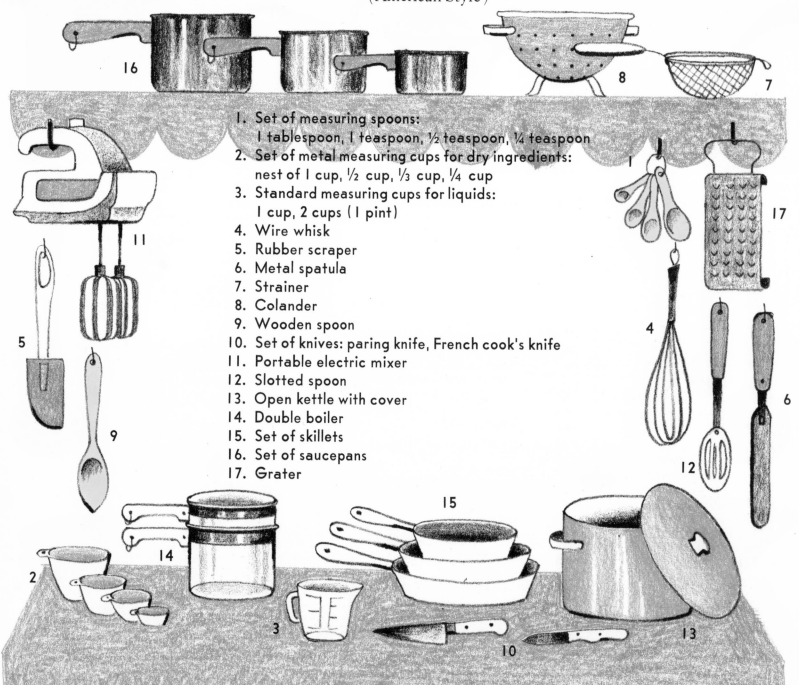

1. Set of measuring spoons:
   1 tablespoon, 1 teaspoon, ½ teaspoon, ¼ teaspoon
2. Set of metal measuring cups for dry ingredients:
   nest of 1 cup, ½ cup, ⅓ cup, ¼ cup
3. Standard measuring cups for liquids:
   1 cup, 2 cups (1 pint)
4. Wire whisk
5. Rubber scraper
6. Metal spatula
7. Strainer
8. Colander
9. Wooden spoon
10. Set of knives: paring knife, French cook's knife
11. Portable electric mixer
12. Slotted spoon
13. Open kettle with cover
14. Double boiler
15. Set of skillets
16. Set of saucepans
17. Grater

KITCHEN UTENSILS Les Ustensiles de Cuisine (French Style)

1. Wooden spoon
2. Spatula
3. Ladle
4. Skimmer
5. Egg beater
6. Saucepan
7. Soup pot
8. Heatproof casserole with cover
9. Skillet
10. Colander
11. Funnel
12. Vegetable mill (for cooked vegetables, purées and soups)
13. Vegetable mill (for raw vegetables)

SOUPS

Les Potages

French soups are all wonderful: from the clear consommés and bouillons, the rich cream soups made with egg yolks and a dash of wine, the chilled soups and the thick vegetable purée-like soups to the hearty stockpot soups made from meat, fowl, or fish stock. Les potages are the pride of the thrifty French house-wife.

Soups are an important part of the French menu. A meal may begin with soup very frequently, sometimes being served at both lunch and dinner. And a simple evening meal for the family may consist entirely of a hearty soup of meat and vegetables.

Following are recipes for a few of the most famous and often-served French soups. The Soupe Fraîche, page 13, is a favorite in summer, made with really ripe tomatoes—ideally, tomatoes fresh from your own garden. You will delight in it!

LEEK AND POTATO SOUP

Soupe aux Poireaux et Pommes de Terre
(For 5 or 6)

Wash leeks, onion and potatoes. Chop leeks finely. Peel and finely chop onion.

Melt butter in kettle. Add leeks and onion; cook, over medium heat, until golden and tender.

Pare potatoes; dice finely. Add to leeks along with chicken broth, salt and pepper.

Bring to boiling; reduce heat and simmer, covered, 20 minutes or until tender.

Press vegetables and broth through sieve or food mill into large saucepan.

Add cream, heat gently, stirring until heated through. Serve in soup bowls.

Note: Reheat any leftover soup the next day; it's even better!

You will need:

Soup kettle
(about 6-quart size)
Sieve or food mill
Large saucepan
Soup bowls

4 leeks
1 medium onion
4 large potatoes
4 tablespoons butter
4 cans (10½-oz. size) chicken broth (about 5⅓ cups)
1 teaspoon salt
⅛ teaspoon pepper
1 cup light cream

You will need:

Medium size heavy saucepan
or heatproof soup tureen

3 large onions
3 tablespoons butter
3 cans (10½ oz.-size)
  condensed beef broth
  Dash pepper (3 turns of the
  pepper mill)
4 thick slices French bread
2 tablespoons grated Parmesan
  cheese
2 triangles (1-oz. size)
  process Gruyère cheese,
  grated

ONION SOUP

Soupe à l'Oignon
(For 4)

Peel onions; slice thinly; measure three cups. Heat butter in soup tureen over medium heat, just until bubbly. Do not burn. Add onion; cook until golden and tender—about ten minutes.

Add beef broth (do not dilute) and pepper. Bring to boiling. Reduce heat; let simmer, covered, 30 minutes.

When soup is nearly finished, toast bread on both sides under broiler. Sprinkle one side of each piece of toast with grated Parmesan cheese, dividing cheese evenly. Then sprinkle with the grated Gruyère cheese. Run under broiler just until cheese is bubbly.

Serve soup right from tureen or pour into four individual bowls. Place toast, cheese side up, on top of soup.

CHICKEN IN THE POT

Poule au Pot
(For 6)

Wash fowl in cold water; dry on paper towels.

In kettle, combine chicken broth, chicken, carrots, leeks, onion, celery, salt, peppercorns, bay leaf, parsley and thyme leaves.

Bring to boiling; reduce heat and simmer, covered, one and a half hours or until chicken is tender.

Lift chicken from broth. Remove chicken from bone and cut into small pieces. Return to broth. Simmer until heated through. Taste for seasoning; add more salt if necessary.

Serve chicken, broth and vegetables in soup bowls. It makes a meal!

You will need:

> **Soup kettle (6-quart size)**
>
> **1 fowl or stewing chicken (about 4 lbs.)**
> **5 cans (10½-oz. size) chicken broth (6⅔ cups)**
> **10 medium size carrots, pared and quartered**
> **3 leeks, cut up**
> **1 onion, peeled and quartered**
> **1 stalk celery, with leaves, cut up**
> **1½ teaspoons salt**
> **6 whole black peppercorns**
> **1 bay leaf, crumbled up**
> **1 parsley sprig**
> **½ teaspoon dried thyme leaves**

You will need:

    Soup kettle (4-quart size)
4 individual soup bowls
    Garlic press
    Sieve

4 large very ripe tomatoes
    (about 3 lbs.)
1 large onion
1 clove garlic
½ tablespoon olive oil
1 bay leaf
1 parsley sprig
½ teaspoon dried thyme leaves
2½ cups water
1½ teaspoons salt
    Dash pepper
    Grated Parmesan cheese

SUMMER SOUP

Soupe Fraîche
(For 4)

To peel tomatoes: Place in boiling water five minutes. Drain; remove skin with knife. Remove seeds; cut tomatoes in quarters.

Peel onion; slice. Peel garlic; put through press.

In soup kettle, heat oil until hot. Add onion and garlic; cook about five minutes or until golden. Add tomatoes, bay leaf, parsley, thyme and water. Cook, uncovered, over medium heat, about one hour. Press vegetables with liquid through a sieve, or better still, combine them all together in a blender.

Return to kettle. Add salt and pepper. Reheat gently until very hot.

Serve in individual bowls; sprinkle with grated Parmesan cheese.

Note: If the soup seems slightly thick, add a little water or white wine. If soup seems slightly acid or sharp in flavor, add a dash of sugar. This soup, like many others, develops flavor if allowed to stand overnight in the refrigerator and then reheated gently before serving.

HORS D'OEUVRES AND FIRST COURSES

Les Hors d'oeuvres et Entrées

The term "hors d'oeuvre" usually means a small dish or two served outside the meal or served as an addition to the menu. These may be hot or cold. More often they are cold.

Hors d'oeuvres may be the little tidbits, familiar to Americans, as served with cocktails. Or they may be side dishes, like vegetables or salads, which the French serve as a first course, but which we like better for a light meal or supper. The Cucumber and Shrimp Salad, Rice Salad and Potato Salad on the following pages are quite typical of this kind of hors d'oeuvre.

In the American menu, we think of the entrée as the main meat or fish course, the principal part of the meal. To the French, an entrée introduces the meal, but is a little fancier and more important than an hors d'oeuvre. For example, a fish dish, a quiche, a soufflé, a pasta, become an entrée when served as a first course, but make a very nice luncheon or supper served all by themselves. The Eggs in Aspic, page 32, or the Coquilles St. Jacques, page 37, would make a very special entrée in the French style for a very special dinner.

POTATO SALAD

Salade de Pommes de Terres
(For 6)

You will need:

Large saucepan with cover
Colander
Large shallow baking dish
Paring knife
Shallow serving dish

6 medium size potatoes
  (about 2 lbs.)
1 teaspoon salt
1 medium onion
1 cup Vinaigrette Sauce*
1 can (7-oz. size) tuna
  Crisp lettuce leaves
2 tablespoons capers, drained
1 tablespoon chopped fresh
  parsley or dill

* Make one cup
  Vinaigrette Sauce, page 50

Scrub potatoes with vegetable brush. Turn into large saucepan. Pour enough boiling water over potatoes to cover them. Add the salt. Cook, covered, over medium heat until potatoes are tender. This will take 25 to 30 minutes. To check for tenderness, pierce potatoes gently with a fork. Drain potatoes in colander. Let cool slightly.

While potatoes are cooking, peel onion and slice thin. Then, using a fork, separate slices into rings. Peel potatoes while they are still warm; cut into slices, about ¼-inch thick.

In baking dish, arrange potato slices in a thin layer, with onion rings over the top. Pour about three-quarters of a cup Vinaigrette Sauce over all. Cover and refrigerate several hours or until well chilled.

Drain tuna and turn into a shallow dish. Cover with one-quarter cup of the Vinaigrette Sauce; refrigerate, covered, along with the potatoes.

At serving time, line a shallow serving bowl with lettuce leaves. Turn potatoes and onions, with the dressing, into bowl. Spoon tuna and dressing evenly over the top. Sprinkle with capers followed by chopped parsley or dill.

STUFFED TOMATOES

Tomates Francfort
(For 4)

Fill saucepan three-fourths full with water. Bring to boiling; reduce heat (water should barely bubble). Add hot dogs or sausage; cook gently eight to ten minutes. Drain and cool.

Cook egg as on page 30. Cool.

Wash and dry tomatoes; cut in half crosswise. With spoon, remove seeds.

Finely chop hot dogs or sausages. Chop egg very fine. Turn into small bowl. Add mayonnaise, lemon juice, parsley, dash of salt and pepper (a few turns of the pepper mill). Toss to mix.

Fill tomatoes with mixture. Decorate each with a lemon slice. Refrigerate several hours or until very well chilled.

Serve on lettuce leaf.

You will need:

Medium saucepan

2 hot dogs or link sausages
1 hard-cooked egg, page 30
2 ripe, medium size tomatoes
3 tablespoons mayonnaise
2 tablespoons lemon juice
1 tablespoon chopped parsley
Salt
Freshly ground pepper
Crisp lettuce leaves
4 slices lemon

RICE SALAD
Salade de Riz
(For 4)

Cook the rice as directed on page 44. Let cool.

Make the Vinaigrette Sauce; add the herbs.

Place the rice in salad bowl with tuna; toss lightly to mix well. Place tomato slices around edge of bowl to make a border. Arrange pimiento, black olives and lemon slices over top. Sprinkle all over with Vinaigrette. Refrigerate until very well chilled—one hour or so. A delicious summer dish.

You will need:

> Large saucepan
> Medium size salad bowl

> 6 tablespoons long grain white rice
> ½ cup Vinaigrette Sauce, page 50
> ½ teaspoon dried tarragon leaves
> 2 tablespoons chopped chives
> 1 can (7-oz. size) tuna, drained
> 2 tomatoes, sliced
> 12 large black olives
> 1 pimiento, thinly sliced
> 3 thin lemon slices

CUCUMBER AND SHRIMP SALAD
Concombre aux Crevettes
(For 4)

You will need:

> Paring knife
> Small bowl, strainer
> Medium size saucepan
> Salad bowl

> 1 medium size cucumber
> 1 tablespoon salt
> ½ lb. medium shrimp, shelled and deveined
> 1 tablespoon shellfish seasoning
> 1 tablespoon heavy cream
> 2 tablespoons lemon juice
> Freshly ground pepper
> 1 or 2 tablespoons chopped fresh chervil,
>   or 1 or 2 teaspoons dried chervil
> Crisp lettuce leaves

Pare cucumbers with paring knife. Slice crosswise very thinly. Turn into a bowl. Sprinkle with the salt; let stand one hour.

In the meantime, fill saucepan with water, three-fourths full. Bring to boiling. Add shrimp and shellfish seasoning. Bring back to boiling and boil, uncovered, three minutes. Shrimp should be nice and tender. Drain shrimp and cool.

Put cucumbers in strainer; rinse under cold running water to remove excess salt. (Taste to see.) Dry on paper towels.

In salad bowl, combine cucumber, shrimp, cream and lemon juice. Add pepper (a few turns of pepper mill). Toss lightly to mix well. Sprinkle top with chervil. Cover and refrigerate for several hours, or until well chilled. Line salad bowl with lettuce leaves for serving.

Trim crusts from bread. Using three tablespoons soft butter, spread each slice with butter on one side only.

Make four sandwiches: On the buttered side of four of the bread slices, place a slice of cheese, then a slice of ham, and top with another slice of cheese. Cover each with a bread slice, buttered side down. Cut each sandwich into quarters.

In skillet, heat two tablespoons butter until bubbly. Arrange little sandwiches in hot butter in single layer, close together. Sauté until golden brown; turn and sauté other side until golden brown and cheese is slightly melted.

Serve as a hot snack with a carbonated drink or as a first course.

GRILLED HAM AND CHEESE SANDWICHES OR CANAPÉS

Croque-Monsieur
(For 4)

You will need:

Large skillet

8 slices white bread
3 tablespoons soft butter
4 thin slices boiled ham
1 pkg. (6 oz.) sliced process
Gruyère cheese (8 slices)
2 tablespoons butter

MEATS

Les Viandes

The French have many wonderful ways to cook meat. Marinated in wine, sautéed in butter, set aflame with cognac, simmered in cream, braised, roasted, flavored with herbs and spiced—they're all delicious!

Even meats like lamb and veal, kidneys and liver, which are not too popular with many Americans, become very palatable, given the French touch. The Veal with Cream, page 24, and the Sautéed Calf's Liver, page 27, are both cases in point. Just be sure that the veal and liver are sliced very thin. Then cook them very quickly over quite high heat. Use a large enough skillet (or two skillets) to sauté them in a single layer. When the slices are nicely browned on each side, they should be sufficiently cooked. Overcooking will make them dry and tough.

The Roast Leg of Lamb, page 26, is a spring lamb, savory with garlic and bay leaves, and roasted until still pink inside, something new for many Americans, who usually roast lamb until it is very well done.

But beef is still the favorite of all in the American cuisine. To roast beef with precision, to broil a steak to perfection, are still "de rigueur" for any cook, French or American.

Roasting and Broiling Guide

Roasting

For roast beef, buy a standing rib or rolled roast, a sirloin roast or an eye of round. It should be "Prime" or "Choice" grade of beef. Then roast it as follows: Place the roast in an open, shallow roasting pan—without a rack if it is a standing rib roast with bones. If it has no bones, place the meat on a rack. The fat side should be on top so that it will baste the meat as it cooks.

Don't add water; don't cover the pan. You may sprinkle the roast with salt and pepper or rub it with a cut clove of garlic.

Beef should be roasted about 20 minutes per pound, in general, but this is not a foolproof guide. The roasting time depends also on the thickness of the meat (diameter or width of the roast), which can vary. Naturally, thin roasts with longer bones will take less time than thicker ones.

Until you become more expert, a meat thermometer can help you, and you will never ruin your roast by overcooking. The roast should be rich brown on the outside and slightly pink on the inside. You can keep the lovers of well done beef happy by giving them the outside slices. Most beef lovers like theirs rare, served "au jus" (with a little of the natural juices of the beef spooned over).

For roasting beef, the following table is a good guide:

Preheat oven to 325° F.

Standing rib roast with bone (width 4½ to 5 inches)	4 lbs.	1¾ hours	Rare
		2¼ hours	Medium
	6 lbs.	3¼ hours	Rare
		3¾ hours	Medium
Sirloin-tip roast	5 lbs.	2½ hours	Rare
		3 hours	Medium

As soon as the roast is cooked, open the oven door and place roasting pan close to the front. If this is not possible (if you are using the oven for other cooking), remove the roast from the oven and cover loosely with foil to keep it warm. You should let the roast stand 20 to 30 minutes before carving. The meat relaxes a bit and will carve better. You will then have time to make gravy or to finish the rest of the dinner.

Broiling

A broiled steak is probably almost everyone's favorite food, but even a good steak can easily be ruined. This is the procedure you should follow: First, heat the broiler. Place the steak on the rack of a lightly greased broiling pan, 3 inches below the heat. (If the steak is more than 1-inch thick, it should be 4 or 5 inches below the heat.)

Broil until top is nicely browned (see table below). Sprinkle with salt and pepper. Turn with tongs, and brown it on the other side. (Do not season broiled meats before cooking as salt draws out the juices.) Steak is delicious served with Béarnaise Sauce, page 49, or with a good mustard.

Sirloin steak	1-inch thick	8 min. per side	Rare
		10 min. per side	Medium
Porterhouse steak	1-inch thick	6 min. per side	Rare
		8 min. per side	Medium
Filet Mignon	1-inch thick	4 min. per side	Rare
		5 min. per side	Medium

LAMB ON SKEWERS

Brochettes
(For 5)

Preheat broiler. Arrange pan so that rack is 6 inches below the heat.

On each skewer, thread four lamb cubes and four pieces of bacon alternately, placing an onion slice and a small piece of bay leaf at the middle of each skewer and at each end.

Brush lamb cubes with oil. Then sprinkle lightly with dried thyme and pepper.

Place the skewers on the rack of the broiler pan. Broil ten to fifteen minutes, turning skewers once so that lamb is nicely browned all over.

Serve at once.

You will need:

5 skewers
(about 8 inches long)
Small brush

1¼ lbs. leg of lamb,
cut into 20 cubes
5 slices bacon, quartered
15 small slices onion
1 tablespoon salad oil
Bay leaves
Dried thyme leaves
Pepper

23

VEAL SCALLOPS WITH CREAM

Escalopes à la Crème
(For 3 or 4)

You will need:

Large skillet

1 lb. *very thin* veal scallops,
  no more than ⅛-inch thick
2 tablespoons butter
½ teaspoon salt
  Dash pepper
¼ cup cognac
¼ cup light cream

Wipe scallops with damp paper towels.

Heat butter in skillet until hot and bubbly. Arrange veal, not overlapping, in butter. Sauté, over medium heat, until golden brown, two to three minutes on each side. While veal is cooking, sprinkle with salt and pepper. (If veal is very thin, it will be cooked through, but if it is still pink inside, cook a minute or two longer.)

Pour cognac over veal; heat slightly; ignite cognac with match. Remove veal to heated serving platter.

Stir cream into pan juices. Stir with wooden spoon until hot. Pour over veal. Serve at once.

PORK CHOPS WITH TOMATO SAUCE

Côtes de Porc Sauce Tomate
(For 4)

You will need:

Medium size heavy skillet with tight fitting cover

4 pork chops, ¾-inch thick (about 1 lb.)
Salt
Pepper
1 small onion, peeled
4 lemon slices, unpeeled
4 tablespoons brown sugar
½ cup catsup
1 small bay leaf, crumbled
⅛ teaspoon dried thyme leaves
1 tablespoon chopped parsley

Wipe chops with damp paper towels. Trim off any excess fat; place these trimmings in the skillet. Heat slowly until fat is melted and hot.

When fat is hot, but not smoking, place chops in skillet, not overlapping. Over medium heat, brown chops, about five minutes on each side, until nicely browned. Remove skillet from heat. Pour off all the fat and discard the trimmings.

Sprinkle chops lightly on each side with salt and pepper.

Cut onion into four slices. On each chop, place a slice of lemon, then top with a slice of onion. Sprinkle each with a tablespoon of brown sugar.

Combine catsup with one-half cup water, bay leaf and thyme; pour into skillet around chops.

Cook chops, covered, over low heat (tomato sauce should bubble slightly) about 45 minutes, until tender. Baste the chops several times during the cooking with the tomato sauce.

Arrange the chops on a heated serving platter; spoon the tomato sauce over the chops. Sprinkle top with chopped parsley.

Preheat oven to 500° F. Wipe lamb with a damp cloth. Place lamb, fat side up, in roasting pan. Insert meat thermometer in thickest part of the meat. Roast lamb, uncovered, 20 minutes.

Reduce oven temperature to 400° F. Sprinkle garlic, carrots, onion, celery and bay leaves over and around the lamb. Roast about 50 minutes longer, or until thermometer registers 165° F. for medium rare, or if you like lamb more well done, 175° F.

Remove lamb to heated serving platter. Keep warm. Pour off drippings (but not vegetables) from roasting pan into bowl. Skim off fat from surface of drippings and discard. Return drippings to roasting pan. Add wine, salt and pepper. Heat to boiling; reduce heat and simmer five minutes. Press vegetables and liquid through strainer into gravy boat. (If sauce seems thick, add a little more wine.)

Slice lamb thinly, crosswise. Serve with sauce.

ROAST LEG OF LAMB

(Delicious for Easter Dinner)
Gigot Rôti
(For 8)

You will need:

Large shallow roasting pan
Meat thermometer
Strainer

1 6-lb. leg of lamb
2 cloves garlic,
    peeled and crushed
2 carrots, pared and cut up
1 small onion,
    peeled and cut up
1 cup diced celery and leaves
2 bay leaves, crushed
1 cup red Burgundy
1 teaspoon salt
Dash pepper

You will need:

Large skillet

3 slices calf's liver, ¼-inch thick (about ¾ lb. in all)
2 tablespoons all-purpose flour
¼ teaspoon salt
Dash pepper
4 tablespoons butter
2 tablespoons lemon juice, freshly squeezed
1 tablespoon chopped parsley

SAUTÉED CALF'S LIVER

Foie de Veau Sauté
(For 3)

Wipe liver with damp paper towels. On a sheet of waxed paper or in a pie plate, combine flour, salt and pepper; mix well.

Dip pieces of liver in flour mixture, coating well on each side. Shake off excess flour.

Heat two tablespoons of the butter in a skillet until very hot; arrange pieces of liver in butter, not overlapping. Sauté quickly over high heat, until browned, two or three minutes; turn and brown other side, two or three minutes. (If you prefer liver quite well done, cook over low heat another minute or two, but, take care, over-cooking will make it tough.)

Place liver on a heated serving platter. Wipe out skillet with paper towels. Heat remaining two tablespoons of butter until bubbly; swirl in lemon juice and chopped parsley; pour over liver. Serve at once.

EGGS AND FISH

Les Oeufs et les Poissons

The French make excellent use of a great variety of fish, many of which are not found in American waters. Fortunately, our native fish can be substituted very successfully in most of the great fish dishes. For example, halibut may be used for turbot; lemon or gray sole substituted for Dover sole or colin; haddock for hake.

You may cook fish in these ways: baking, broiling, sautéeing, frying and poaching. But always remember this—fish requires only a short cooking time. Overcooking can make it dry and tough. Fish is sufficiently cooked if it "flakes" or separates easily when tested with a fork or the point of a knife.

Fish is as nourishing as meat, but much more varied in taste, and best of all, many doctors recommend it instead of meat!

And now, for eggs. As one of the main ingredients in cooking, eggs form the basis for many recipes. They are quickly and easily prepared, but nevertheless, have great character and thus are always welcomed by last minute guests. One of the omelets, page 31, would be just right and delicious for unexpected company!

Here are a few words of advice about cooking eggs: Always use low or moderate heat. Too high or prolonged heat will make eggs tough and rubbery.

Don't try to beat egg whites if there is any yolk in them. Carefully remove any bits of yolk with paper towels before beating. Bring egg whites to room temperature before beating them. They will then give better volume. You will find these last two points particularly helpful in making soufflés and many desserts.

EGGS

Les Oeufs

There are six basic ways to cook eggs. When you have mastered these, you will be able to make easily the many dishes in which eggs are used.

HARD-COOKED EGGS *Oeufs Durs*

Gently place eggs in a large saucepan with a cover. Add water to a level 1-inch above eggs. Over high heat, bring to boiling. Remove pan from heat; cover tightly; let stand 20 minutes. Pour off hot water; cool eggs at once in cold water. This prevents darkening of egg yolks and shells will come off easily.

SOFT-COOKED EGGS *Oeufs à la Coque*

Follow the directions above for hard-cooked eggs, but let eggs stand for only three or four minutes after removing from heat, depending upon how you like them. Cool under cold water at once to stop the cooking, but not enough to make them cold inside.

FRIED EGGS *Oeufs sur le Plat*

Over low heat, melt 1 tablespoon (standard measure) butter for each egg to be fried. Heat until butter is bubbly, not browned. Break eggs, one at a time, directly into pan. Cook slowly five minutes, or until whites are firm. Sprinkle with a little salt and pepper. Carefully remove with broad spatula to serving plate.

POACHED EGGS *Oeufs Pochés*

Fill a large skillet with water, at least 1-inch deep. Bring to boiling, then reduce heat to simmer. Break each egg into a saucer. One by one, quickly slip each egg into water. Cook covered, over low heat, three to five minutes, or until the white is firm. Lift out with slotted spoon. Drain well.

SCRAMBLED EGGS *Oeufs Brouillés*

Allow 1 teaspoon milk for each egg. Thoroughly mix together eggs and milk and salt and pepper to taste. Heat butter (enough to cover bottom of skillet) until just hot enough so that a drop of water will sizzle. Pour in egg mixture, and reduce heat. When eggs have set slightly, stir constantly with a fork. Perfectly scrambled eggs should be soft and creamy. Don't overcook.

Before cooking scrambled eggs you might add: grated cheese, chopped herbs, sautéed chopped mushrooms or cooked chopped chicken livers.

OMELET *Oeufs en Omelette* (Makes one omelet)

In a small bowl, break 3 eggs; add a dash of salt and pepper. Beat with a fork or wire whisk just until yolks and whites are blended. Eggs should not be foamy.

Heat an omelet pan or a heavy, 9-inch skillet over low heat. (Pan is hot enough when a drop of water sizzles and rolls off surface.) Add 1 tablespoon butter and let it melt; it should not brown.

Quickly turn eggs into skillet. Cook, over medium heat, several minutes. As omelet cooks, run spatula around edge of pan to loosen. Tilt pan; let uncooked egg run underneath.

Omelet is done when it is golden brown on the bottom and there is no longer any uncooked egg on top.

To turn out omelet: Loosen edge with spatula. Fold over to edge of pan and tilt out on plate. This takes a little practice!

HERB OMELET *Omelette aux Fines Herbes*

Before cooking omelet, add to the eggs 1 tablespoon dried fines herbes mixture, right from the jar. Continue as above.

Use your imagination to vary the fillings for omelets. You can use leftover cooked vegetables, like spinach, broccoli, asparagus; chopped cooked ham or chicken; all kinds of grated cheeses; jelly; or combinations of these ingredients. You need never have the same omelet twice!

EGGS IN ASPIC

Oeufs en Gelée
(For 4)

Fill medium saucepan, three-fourths full, with water. With large spoon, gently lower eggs, one at a time, into water. Bring water to boiling over high heat.

Take pan off heat at once. Cover; let stand three minutes, no longer. Pour off water. Run cold water over eggs to stop the cooking. (Eggs must not be overcooked. They should be soft in center.)

Sprinkle gelatine over one-half cup consommé in small saucepan. Let stand five minutes to soften, then melt gelatine, stirring, over low heat.

Add remainder of can of consommé, lemon juice, vinegar and salt. Mix well. Refrigerate until cool and slightly thickened, but not set, about 15 minutes.

While gelatine is cooling, carefully remove shells from eggs. Cut ham into four pieces.

Spoon one tablespoon cooled gelatine mixture into the bottom of each mold. Then arrange a sprig of tarragon or watercress on top.

Place an egg in the center of each mold. Then place a slice of ham on top. Pour gelatine mixture over each mold to cover egg and ham completely. Refrigerate until firm— about one hour.

To unmold: Run a spatula or knife around the edge of each mold to loosen. Invert on individual serving plate. Gently shake out. Garnish with watercress.

You will need:

Medium size saucepan
Small saucepan
4 (6-oz. size) custard cups
   or oval molds

4 eggs
1 envelope unflavored gelatine
1 can (12½-oz. size)
   chicken consommé (1¾ cups)
¼ cup lemon juice
2 teaspoons tarragon vinegar
¼ teaspoon salt
   Tarragon leaves
   or watercress
1 thin slice of cooked ham

FISH
Les Poissons

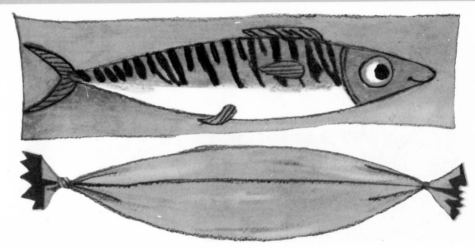

MACKEREL IN FOIL (*without any odor!*)

Maquereaux en Papillotes (pas d'odeur!)
(For 4)

You will need:

Small saucepan
Large shallow baking dish
4 large pieces aluminum foil

4 medium size mackerel
(about ½ lb. each)
¼ cup butter
1 large shallot, peeled
and finely chopped
¼ cup lemon juice
1 teaspoon salt
⅛ teaspoon pepper

Preheat oven to 350° F.

Have the man in the fish store clean the mackerel and remove the heads and tails.

Wash the mackerel under cold running water. Dry well on paper towels.

Wrap each mackerel loosely in a piece of foil.

Place in baking dish. Bake 15 minutes.

While mackerel is baking, melt butter in small saucepan; add chopped shallot; cook several minutes, being careful not to burn the butter. Add lemon juice.

Test mackerel with a fork; fish is sufficiently cooked when it flakes easily. Do not overcook.

Gently remove fish from foil to serving dish.

Sprinkle with salt and pepper. Pour butter sauce over the top. Serve at once.

If you do not like mackerel, you may substitute trout, bass, halibut or snapper.

LITTLE FISH-FRY
Petite Friture
(For 6)

Have the man in the fish store clean the smelts, asking him to leave the heads and tails on.

Wash them well in cold running water, then drain well on paper towels.

Over medium heat, start heating the oil in heavy skillet.

Combine the cup of milk and one teaspoon salt in a shallow dish. Add smelts; let them soak three minutes, then roll them in the flour on waxed paper.

If you have a deep-frying thermometer, put it in the oil (the bottom of the thermometer should not touch the bottom of the pan). The oil should be at 300° F.

When oil is at the right temperature, turn heat down slightly—oil should not smoke. You will need to keep checking the temperature of the oil so that it does not cool down too much or become too hot.

Plunge fish into the hot oil (eight or ten at a time). Let them cook six to ten minutes, depending upon their size. They should be a nice golden brown.

Lift out with a slotted spoon. Drain on crumpled paper towels. Sprinkle with salt. Keep warm in a low oven while frying the rest.

Arrange fish on a heated serving platter; surround with lemon.

You will need:

Large deep heavy skillet
or large kettle
Shallow dish
Slotted spoon

2 lbs. smelts
1½ pints oil for deep-frying
1 cup milk
1 teaspoon salt
⅔ cup all-purpose flour
2 lemons, quartered
lengthwise

POACHED SLICED WHITING

Tranches de Colin en Court-Bouillon
(For 4)

In saucepan, bring water to boiling. Add vinegar, salt, pepper, onion, shallots, carrot, thyme, bay leaf and one sprig parsley. Let simmer, uncovered, about three-quarters of an hour. Refrigerate until cold.

To poach the fish: Wipe slices of fish with dampened paper towels. Place fish in chilled stock. Over medium heat, bring stock just to boiling point. Turn down heat at once and let simmer very gently. (Fish must never boil.) Poach fish, uncovered, about three to five minutes. Be careful not to overcook.

Lift out with skimmer or slotted spoon. Drain fish on paper towels. Arrange on warm serving platter; pour melted butter over fish; decorate each end of platter with lemon slices and parsley.

Note: If you prefer, you may substitute sole for whiting.

You will need:

Large saucepan
Skimmer or slotted spoon
Paper toweling

2 pints water
½ cup tarragon vinegar
2 tablespoons salt
⅛ teaspoon pepper
1 large onion, peeled
2 shallots, peeled
1 carrot, pared
1 teaspoon dried thyme leaves
1 bay leaf
1 sprig parsley
4 slices whiting (1½ lbs.)
¼ cup butter, melted
4 slices lemon
Parsley, for garnish

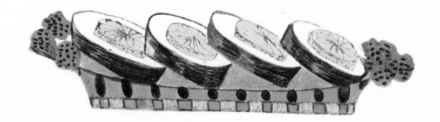

FILLETS OF SOLE IN BUTTER
Filets de Sole au Beurre
(For 4)

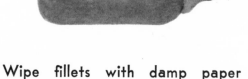

Wipe fillets with damp paper towels.

Turn flour into a shallow dish. Dip fillets, one by one, into flour to coat nicely on each side. Gently shake off any excess flour.

Heat butter in skillet over medium heat just until melted and bubbly. It should not smoke. Place fish fillets in butter, not overlapping. Sauté over low heat, four minutes on each side. Fish should be a golden color.

Remove with broad spatula to a hot serving platter. Sprinkle with lemon juice, parsley, salt and pepper. Garnish platter with lemon slices.

Note: You may use fillet of whiting instead of sole.

You will need:

    Large heavy skillet
    Shallow dish

    4 fillets of sole (about 1½ lbs.)
    2 or 3 tablespoons flour
    ¼ cup butter
    2 tablespoons lemon juice
    1 tablespoon chopped parsley
    ½ teaspoon salt
    ⅛ teaspoon pepper
    4 slices lemon

SCALLOPS AND MUSHROOMS IN WHITE WINE SAUCE

Coquilles Saint-Jacques
(For 4)

You will need:

Medium saucepan
Slotted spoon
Strainer
4 individual ramekins
or scallop shells

½ cup dry white wine
1 onion, quartered
1 shallot, coarsely chopped
1 bay leaf
4 whole black peppercorns
¼ teaspoon salt
1 lb. sea scallops
2 tablespoons butter
1 onion finely chopped
¼ lb. mushrooms, sliced
¼ cup flour
¼ cup milk
½ cup light cream
½ cup grated Gruyère cheese
¼ cup packaged
dry bread crumbs
1 tablespoon butter, melted

In saucepan, combine one-half cup white wine, the quartered onion, shallot, bay leaf, whole black peppercorns and salt. Bring to boiling; add scallops, simmer, covered, five or six minutes or until tender.

With slotted spoon, lift scallops from liquid; set aside. Strain liquid and save for later use. Discard vegetables.

Preheat oven to 375° F.

Heat two tablespoons butter in same saucepan. Add chopped onion and mushrooms. Sauté until tender—about five minutes.

Remove saucepan from heat. Blend in flour. Gradually stir in milk and cream.

Return to heat. Bring to boiling, stirring; reduce heat and simmer, stirring often, until quite thick—about five minutes. Add grated cheese; stir, over low heat, until cheese is melted.

Remove from heat. Gradually stir in liquid reserved from scallops. (This should measure one-half cup; if it does not, add enough white wine to make up the difference.) Add scallops.

Turn mixture into scallop shells or ramekins; place on cookie sheet. Toss dry bread crumbs with one tablespoon heated butter. Sprinkle evenly over scallops. Bake ten to fifteen minutes, until nicely browned on top.

VEGETABLES

Les Légumes

Once you know how to prepare vegetables well, as the French do, you will love them all. Here are some general rules:

1) The French have long advocated waterless (or almost waterless) cooking for vegetables. Most fresh vegetables should be cooked in 1-inch of gently boiling water with ½ teaspoon of salt. Use a heavy saucepan with a tight fitting cover. Cook just until they are tender when pierced with a fork. Take care not to over-cook them. (The flavor, color and even the vitamins in vegetables are destroyed by overcooking.)

2) Try to evaporate most of the cooking liquid by the time the vegetables are cooked. If any liquid remains, do not discard it, for you will be throwing away some of the vitamins as well. Instead, use it to make soups and gravies.

3) Season vegetables carefully, and butter them liberally. Then sprinkle them with herbs, such as thyme, chervil, tarragon or basil; or a spice like nutmeg; or a dash of lemon juice. A great treat with broccoli or asparagus is Hollandaise Sauce, page 51. This sauce is also delicious on green beans, cauliflower, or stirred into spinach.

The French have a way with salads, too. For a really good, crisp salad:

1) Wash salad greens as soon as you bring them home from the market. Place them in a salad basket or colander and wash in cold running water several times. Then dry them gently, but very well, on paper towels and place them in the re-frigerator crisper. They will be crisp in an hour or two. If you do this, your greens will always be clean, crisp, dry and ready to use when you want them.

2) Prepare the Vinaigrette Sauce, page 50, ahead of time in the salad bowl. Just before serving, break crisp salad greens in bite-size pieces into salad bowl, right on top of the dressing. Toss well and serve. Never add greens to salad dress-ing until serving time as they will wilt if they are mixed with the dressing too soon.

FRENCH FRIED POTATOES
Pommes de Terre Frites
(For 4)

You will need:

An electric deep-fat fryer
or an electric skillet

2 lbs. white potatoes
6 cups salad oil (less if you are
using an electric skillet)
1 tablespoon salt

Wash and pare potatoes using a paring knife or potato peeler. Dry potatoes well on paper towels.

Cut potatoes lengthwise into quarters, then cut potatoes again to make rectangles.

In deep-fat fryer or electric skillet, slowly heat oil; it should not smoke. Temperature should be kept at 425° F., or as manufacturer directs.

Drop the potatoes in the oil (half the potatoes at a time); fry about eight minutes. Potatoes should be cooked and tender, but pale in color. Drain potatoes on crumpled paper towels. Cook remaining potatoes. Set aside.

Just before serving, reheat oil. Add the potatoes; cook until nicely browned. Drain on paper towels; sprinkle lightly with salt. Serve at once.

POTATOES MOUSSELINE (Extra Special Mashed Potatoes)
Pommes de Terre Mousseline
(For 6)

You will need:

Paring knife or potato peeler
Chopping board
Large saucepan with
tight fitting cover
Potato masher or
portable electric mixer
Small saucepan
Small bowl

2 lbs. white potatoes
1 teaspoon salt
1 cup milk
1 egg, separated
2 tablespoons butter
Freshly ground pepper

Wash potatoes; pare with paring knife or potato peeler. Cut potatoes into quarters. Turn into large saucepan.

Pour on boiling water—enough just to cover potatoes; add salt. Bring to boiling, then lower the heat and gently simmer the potatoes, covered, about 25 minutes, until they are tender when pierced with a fork.

When potatoes are tender, drain well, and return them to saucepan. Mash with a potato masher or beat, at medium speed, with a portable electric mixer until smooth (no lumps!).

In small saucepan, heat the milk over a low flame. Also, in small bowl, beat egg white just until stiff.

Then, add the butter to the potatoes. Place over very low heat. Add the hot milk, a little at a time, beating with a wooden spoon until light and fluffy.

Beat in the egg yolk and dash of pepper. Lastly, blend in the beaten egg white until nicely combined. Taste, adding more salt and pepper, and butter, if you like.

Turn into a heated serving dish, mounding up high.

GREEN BEANS
Haricots Verts
(For 4)

Place 2 pounds green beans in colander; wash in cold water; drain. With paring knife, trim off the ends; remove strings, if any.

Fill a medium size saucepan, three-fourths full of water. Add ½ teaspoon salt. Bring to boiling; add green beans; bring back to boiling; reduce heat and boil gently 25 minutes—uncovered, to keep the green color of the beans. Drain beans.

In a large skillet, melt 4 tablespoons butter. When butter is foamy, add the beans; sauté over medium heat ten minutes, stirring several times. Add 1 tablespoon chopped fresh parsley and a dash of pepper; toss to combine and serve at once.

ENDIVE IN BUTTER
Endives au Beurre
(For 4)

Fill the saucepan half-full of water. Bring to boiling.

While water is heating, wash and dry endive. Peel off any outer wilted leaves.

Put endive in boiling water along with lemon juice. Let stand uncovered ten minutes to blanch endive.

Drain endive well, being careful not to break it.

Melt butter in same saucepan. Add endive. Cook gently, uncovered, to evaporate water, until very hot and coated with butter—about 30 minutes until endive is tender but not falling apart. Sprinkle very lightly with fresh black pepper (a turn or two of the pepper mill).

You will need:

   Large, heavy saucepan

2 lbs. endive
2 tablespoons lemon juice
   Dash of freshly ground pepper
4 tablespoons butter

MACARONI AND CHEESE
Macaroni au Gratin
(For 4)

Fill saucepan with three quarts cold water; add salt. Bring to boiling, covered.

Add macaroni to boiling water; bring back to boiling; then reduce heat so that macaroni boils gently, uncovered, for 20 minutes.

Preheat oven to 425° F., and make White Sauce, page 48, while macaroni is cooking.

Taste macaroni; when tender, drain very well in colander.

Sprinkle bottom of baking dish with most of the bread crumbs. (Save several tablespoons to sprinkle over the top.)

Arrange macaroni over the crumbs; spoon White Sauce over macaroni; sprinkle with grated cheese and pepper (several turns of the pepper mill).

Sprinkle the reserved crumbs over the top.

Put in oven and bake 15 minutes or until cheese is melted and top is golden.

You will need:

Large saucepan or kettle
Colander
Shallow baking dish
(12 x 8 x 2 inches)

1 tablespoon salt
2 cups White Sauce, page 48
½ cup packaged
　dry bread crumbs
½ lb. elbow macaroni
¼ lb. Gruyère or
　Cheddar cheese, grated
Freshly ground pepper

CRÉOLE RICE

Riz à la Créole

(For 2 or 3)

Fill saucepan three-fourths full with water. Add salt. Bring to boiling over high heat.

Wash the rice in warm water in a bowl four times to eliminate excess starch.

When water boils, add washed rice; boil hard, uncovered. After ten minutes taste rice. Cook until rice is tender, but still firm and not mushy.

Preheat oven to 300° F.

Strain rice. Rinse under cold water. Turn out onto a heatproof serving dish. Add butter and pepper (several turns of the pepper mill).

Heat rice in oven, stirring occasionally, ten minutes or until heated through.

You will need:

Large saucepan
Strainer
Heatproof serving dish

3 tablespoons long grain white rice
1 teaspoon salt
2 tablespoons butter
Freshly ground pepper

You will need:

Large skillet
Spatula
Small skillet
Small bowl

1 cup raw long grain rice
¼ cup salad oil
¼ chopped green scallions
1½ tablespoons soy sauce
Dash of salt
Dash of pepper
2 eggs

CHINESE-STYLE RICE

Riz Cantonnais
(For 4)

Cook rice according to the directions on the package label. Refrigerate until very cold, overnight if possible. (Or if you have three cups of cold leftover rice, you may use it.)

Heat three tablespoons oil in large skillet. When oil is hot, but not smoking, add rice and cook, turning frequently with spatula to coat rice with oil and to heat through.

Add scallions, soy sauce, salt and pepper. Mix gently to blend. Keep warm over low heat.

At the same time, break eggs into small bowl. Add one tablespoon water, dash of pepper. With a fork, beat eggs —just to mix well, not foamy.

In a small skillet, heat one tablespoon salad oil until hot. Add eggs; cook, over low heat, stirring with fork just until set, but still soft. Toss lightly with rice. Serve at once.

THE SAUCES

Les Sauces

In the French cuisine, the sauce always complements and enhances the food with which it is to be served. The sauce must be light, smooth, delicately seasoned and perfectly blended.

Sauces may be hot or cold, sweet or savory, but certain sauces are basic to all others. When you have mastered the basic ones, you will be able to make the many sauces that are variations of them.

The Hollandaise Sauce, page 51, is one of the basic types. It is an emulsion, made with egg yolks, butter (or oil) and lemon juice (or vinegar). Mayonnaise and Béarnaise Sauce, page 49, belong to this family. Both the Hollandaise and the Béarnaise must be cooked over hot water, in a double boiler. They are tricky to do, and if cooked too long or at too high a heat, they will curdle.

The Sauce Blanche, page 48, is another basic type. Since it is a sauce made with flour, it is important that it be brought just to the boiling point so that the flour is completely cooked and will not give the sauce a "raw" taste. The Sauce Mornay, page 49, belongs to this group.

If you follow the directions for making these sauces very carefully, you should have no difficulty.

WHITE SAUCE
Sauce Blanche
(Makes I cup)

Melt butter in saucepan. Remove pan from heat. Stir in flour, salt and pepper. Then gradually stir in milk.

Over medium heat, bring to boiling, stirring. Reduce heat and let sauce cook one minute. This is a medium-thick white sauce. It is a basic sauce for many others.

Add one-quarter cup chopped parsley and two tablespoons lemon juice just before serving. This is delicious over vegetables or fish. Or you can add one tablespoon horseradish and one teaspoon lemon juice before serving, to make a very nice sauce for corned beef or boiled beef.

You will need:

Medium size saucepan
Wooden spoon

2 tablespoons butter
2 tablespoons all-purpose flour
½ teaspoon salt
Dash pepper
1 cup milk

BÉARNAISE SAUCE

Sauce Béarnaise
(For 4)

In saucepan, combine tarragon vinegar with white wine, tarragon and chopped shallots. Over medium heat, bring just to boiling. Reduce heat and simmer, uncovered, to reduce liquid to about two tablespoons. This will take five minutes or so.

Pour vinegar mixture through a small strainer into the top of a double boiler. With wire whisk, beat in two egg yolks. Cook, over hot water, beating until sauce thickens. Gradually add butter, a tablespoon at a time, beating to melt. Sauce should be the consistency of mayonnaise.

Serve Béarnaise Sauce warm or cold with broiled steak or lamb chops.

You will need:

Small saucepan
Wire whisk
Double boiler

2 tablespoons tarragon vinegar
2 tablespoons dry white wine
1 tablespoon chopped
   fresh tarragon or
1 teaspoon dried
   tarragon leaves
2 teaspoons finely chopped
   shallots
2 egg yolks
¼ cup butter

MORNAY SAUCE

Sauce Mornay
(Makes 1½ cups)

Make Mornay Sauce by first making the White Sauce on the opposite page.

Then grate Gruyère, Swiss or Cheddar cheese to measure 1 cup. Add cheese and ¼ teaspoon dry mustard to the White Sauce.

Cook, stirring, over low heat, until cheese is melted and sauce is hot.

Mornay Sauce goes very well over cauliflower, broccoli or asparagus.

You will need:

Salad bowl
Salad server

½ teaspoon salt
¼ teaspoon pepper
½ teaspoon dry mustard
2 tablespoons wine vinegar
2 tablespoons olive oil
   or other salad oil

VINAIGRETTE SAUCE

Sauce Vinaigrette
(For 4 or 5)

In bottom of salad bowl, put the salt, pepper, mustard and vinegar. Stir until salt is dissolved. Add oil, beating well with a fork to mix thoroughly.

Add five cups crisp mixed salad greens, broken into bite-size pieces. Toss with salad fork and spoon until well combined. Serve at once.

Variations on Sauce Vinaigrette

For a creamier dressing, mash one hard-cooked egg yolk with a fork in salad bowl with the salt, pepper and mustard. Add two tablespoons of lemon juice and then the oil as directed above.

You might like to add some chopped tarragon, parsley or chives, to your taste.

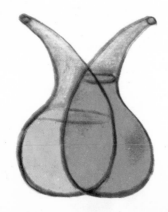

HOLLANDAISE SAUCE

Sauce Hollandaise
(For 6)

In top of double boiler or in a small bowl, beat 3 egg yolks slightly, using a wire whisk or a fork. Beat in, several drops at a time, 1/3 cup melted butter. Then gradually add 1/3 cup boiling water, beating constantly.

Cook, stirring constantly, over hot water (if not using double boiler, set bowl over hot water) until thickened.

Remove from hot water. Add ¼ teaspoon salt. Gradually stir in 2 tablespoons lemon juice. Keep warm over hot water until serving, or serve cold.

Serve with artichokes, asparagus, cauliflower, green beans, broccoli, cold chicken or fish.

THE DESSERTS

Les Desserts

Bombe, crême, crêpe, éclair, gâteau, glace, meringue, mousse, patisserie, tarte, soufflé—so many wonderful desserts to master.

These are the most exciting creations of the French cuisine and perhaps the most difficult. In making desserts, follow directions precisely, as each is a scientific experiment, and one little change may throw it off.

Here are a few words of advice :

In the Tartes aux Fruits, page 54, we advise that the pastry be pressed into the tart pans with the fingers. This is a very rich cookie-dough pastry and difficult to handle. If you try to roll it out, you may make it dry and tough.

The Crêpes, page 58, are really rich, thin pancakes. It's important to refrigerate the batter (the longer the better—even overnight). It will then be smoother and creamier. When you have mastered the making of crêpes, you may go to crêpes Suzette (crêpes in a flaming orange sauce), a spectacular dessert and the specialty of many great restaurants.

In making Nougatine, page 59, the melting or caramelizing of the sugar can be tricky. If it turns a very dark amber color, it will have an unpleasant burnt-sugar flavor. If it is a very light color, it will have little flavor and no character at all. But a golden amber color will give just the right caramel taste.

In the Meringues, page 60, it is important to beat the egg whites until stiff and to beat in the sugar gradually until the mixture is very stiff. The Meringues will then hold their shape and be nice and crisp when they are baked.

Although your first attempts at desserts may produce somewhat less than perfect-looking results, your creations are sure to taste delicious.

FRUIT TARTS

Tartes aux Fruits
(Makes 8 small tarts)

You will need:

Medium bowl
Fork
8 (3-inch size) tart pans
Wire rack
Saucepan
Small bowl
Rotary egg beater

PASTRY FOR TART SHELLS

¼ cup butter
2 tablespoons sugar
Dash salt
1 egg yolk
1 cup unsifted, all-purpose flour

FILLING

Fruit of your choice:
strawberries, apricot halves,
sliced bananas, pitted
cherries, pineapple tidbits,
blueberries

Apricot preserves
½ cup heavy cream

In medium bowl, with fork, blend butter, sugar, salt and egg yolk until smooth and well combined. Gradually stir in flour, mixing until smooth. With your fingers, using about two tablespoons dough for each tart, gently press dough into the tart pans, lining bottoms and sides evenly. (You may roll out the dough on a lightly-floured surface to slightly more than 1/8-inch thickness. You will find it easier to pat the dough gently into the pans.)

Refrigerate on cookie sheet until thoroughly chilled—at least one hour.

Preheat oven to 375° F.

Prick tart shells all over with fork. Bake about 15 minutes or until golden. Let cool in pans on wire rack. Then very carefully loosen edge of tart shells from pans with the tip of a knife, and remove from pans. Just before serving, fill with the fruit you like best. Make a pretty assortment.

Spoon about one-half cup apricot preserves into a small saucepan. Melt over low heat.

Drizzle melted preserves over fruit to glaze top.

In small bowl, beat cream with rotary beater just until cream mounds and holds its shape. Do not over beat. Spoon on tarts.

FRUIT CAKE

Cake aux Fruits
(1 loaf cake)

You will need:

- A 9 x 5 x 3-inch loaf pan
- Brown wrapping paper
- Electric mixer with
- large mixing bowl
- Wooden spoon,
- Rubber scraper
- Wire cake rack
- Cheesecloth
- Cake tester
- or wooden toothpick

- ½ cup butter
- 1 cup sugar
- ½ teaspoon almond extract
- 4 eggs
- 2 cups sifted all-purpose flour
- 1¼ cups light raisins
- 1 jar (4-oz. size) candied cherries
- 1 jar (4-oz. size) chopped candied citron
- Sherry

Preheat oven to 325° F. Lightly grease loaf pan. Line bottom and sides of pan with brown paper; grease paper well.

Let ½ cup butter soften in large electric mixer bowl. At medium speed, beat butter until fluffy; gradually beat in sugar until very light and fluffy. Add almond extract.

Beat in eggs, one at a time, beating well after each is added.

With wooden spoon, stir in flour—just until combined. Then stir in raisins, cherries, and citron. Mix until well combined. Turn into prepared pan, scraping bowl with rubber scraper.

Bake from one and a quarter to one and a half hours, or until a cake tester or a wooden pick inserted near the center comes out clean.

Let cool in pan one-half hour; then turn out onto wire cake rack; gently remove brown paper; let cake cool completely.

Wrap in cheesecloth soaked in sherry, then in plastic film or foil, and store in a tightly covered tin several days before serving.

Serve thinly cut slices.

CHERRY CAKE

Clafouti
(For 8)

Preheat oven to 350° F.

With one tablespoon melted butter, lightly grease bottom of baking dish. Put cherries in strainer to drain. Turn drained cherries into bottom of baking dish.

Combine one-quarter cup sugar and cinnamon; sprinkle over fruit, then drizzle with three tablespoons melted butter.

Make cake batter: Sift flour with one-half cup sugar, baking powder and salt into medium bowl.

Beat egg slightly with fork. Add to flour mixture along with milk, one-quarter cup melted butter and vanilla extract. Beat vigorously with wooden spoon until smooth and well blended—about two minutes.

Pour batter over the cherries. Bake 35 to 40 minutes or until cake is golden brown and top springs back when gently pressed with fingertip.

Loosen cake from edge of baking dish with small spatula, but do not remove from baking dish.

Turn cake upside down* on serving platter. Let cool slightly. Then remove baking dish. Serve cake warm with vanilla ice cream or whipped cream.

* Clafouti is not really an upside down cake. However, it comes very close to the American version.

You will need:

1½-quart (8½-inch) shallow round baking dish
Strainer
Medium bowl
Small spatula

TOPPING
4 tablespoons butter, melted
1 can (1-lb., 1-oz. size) pitted, dark sweet cherries
¼ cup light brown sugar, packed
1 teaspoon cinnamon
Vanilla ice cream
or whipped cream

CAKE BATTER
1 cup sifted all-purpose flour
½ cup sugar
1½ teaspoons baking powder
½ teaspoon salt
¼ cup butter, melted
1 egg
⅓ cup milk
1 teaspoon vanilla extract

CRÊPES
(For 4 or 5)

In small electric mixer bowl, combine eggs, milk, flour, salt and oil.

Beat at medium speed, until smooth.

Refrigerate batter, covered, at least one hour.

To cook crêpes: For each crêpe, melt ¼ teaspoon butter in skillet. Pour in about two tablespoons batter, rotating pan quickly, to spread batter completely over bottom of pan. The crêpes must be very thin.

Cook over medium heat, until lightly browned on underside; turn with spatula and brown other side. Stack crêpes, browned side up, as taken from skillet. Keep warm, in a very low oven while making the rest.

To serve: Spread warm crêpes (lighter side) with strawberry jam. Roll up; sprinkle with confectioners' sugar. Arrange on serving platter. Beat cream in small bowl with rotary beater just until stiff. Serve with crêpes.

Makes eight or nine crêpes.

You will need:

Electric mixer with small bowl
Skillet (7-inch size)
Spatula
Rotary beater

2 eggs
½ cup milk
¼ cup unsifted all-purpose flour
Dash salt
1 teaspoon salad oil
Butter
Strawberry preserves
Confectioners' sugar
¼ cup heavy cream

LITTLE NOUGATS

Nougatine
(Makes ¾ lb.)

Grease the large dish very well with butter. Turn hazelnuts into dish, arranging evenly over bottom.

In skillet, combine sugar, corn syrup and one-quarter cup water. Let cook, uncovered, over very low heat, without stirring, until syrup turns a light golden-amber color—40 to 50 minutes. Do not stir.

Remove from heat.

Immediately pour hot caramel syrup over hazelnuts. Refrigerate until hard—at least one hour.

Turn out of pie plate; break into pieces with a heavy spoon.

You will need:

   **Large shallow dish
   (10 to 12 inches)
   Large heavy skillet
   (9-inch size)**

   **1 teaspoon butter
   About 30 hazelnuts, shelled
   and broken into pieces (¼ cup)
   1 cup sugar
   2 tablespoons light corn syrup
¼ cup water**

You will need:

    Electric mixer with small bowl
    Cookie sheet
    Brown wrapping paper
    Rubber scraper
    Large spoon
    Spatula
    Wire rack

  2 egg whites
    Dash salt
½ cup fine granulated sugar
⅛ teaspoon vanilla extract
    Green and red food color
    (optional)

MERINGUES (Makes 24)

Let egg whites warm to room temperature in small bowl of electric mixer—about one hour.

Lightly grease cookie sheet. Cut brown wrapping paper to fit cookie sheet. Place on cookie sheet; lightly grease paper.

Heat oven to 275° F.

With mixer at high speed, beat egg whites with salt until whites are very stiff.

Gradually beat in three-fourths of the sugar, beating until very stiff. Using a rubber scraper, fold in the rest of the sugar and vanilla until well combined.

Divide meringue mixture in half. Fold three drops red food coloring into one half, and three drops green food coloring into the other half. You may omit the color if you like.

Using large spoon, drop in 24 mounds, not too close together, onto the brown paper on the cookie sheet. Bake 25 minutes or until meringues are dry on the surface.

With spatula, remove meringues from the paper while they are still warm. Let cool on wire rack.

Serve meringues on top of ice cream, or put a scoop of ice cream between two meringues.

You can store meringues in a tightly covered tin for several weeks.

You will need:

   1 quart-size baking dish
   Electric mixer with
   large mixer bowl
   Rubber scraper
   Spatula

   3 egg whites
   2 jars (15-oz. size) applesauce
   ½ teaspoon cinnamon
   6 tablespoons granulated sugar
   2 tablespoons
   confectioners' sugar

APPLESAUCE MERINGUE
Pommes Meringuées
(For 6)

Let egg whites warm to room temperature in large bowl of electric mixer—it will take about an hour. The egg whites will give better volume when beaten.

Preheat oven to 375° F.

Turn applesauce into baking dish. Stir cinnamon into applesauce to mix well.

At high speed, beat egg whites until soft peaks form when the beater is slowly raised.

Gradually beat in granulated sugar; beat just until stiff peaks form.

Spread meringue evenly over applesauce, then make pretty swirls with the spatula. Sprinkle top evenly with confectioners' sugar.

Bake 12 to 15 minutes or until meringue is slightly golden and crusty.

Serve warm.

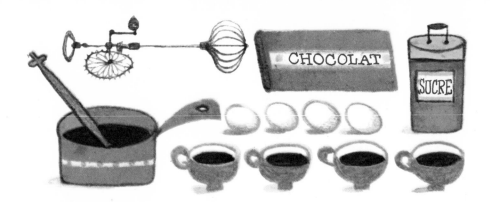

You will need:

Electric mixer with large bowl
Double boiler
Rotary beater
Several small bowls
Wooden spoon
Wire whisk
Serving bowl or 4 small soufflé dishes

3 egg whites
5 egg yolks
¼ cup sugar
¼ cup rum (light or dark)
½ pkg. (8-oz. size) semisweet chocolate squares (4)
¼ cup sugar
Whipped cream

CHOCOLATE MOUSSE

Mousse au Chocolat

(For 4)

Let egg whites warm to room temperature—about one hour—in large bowl of electric mixer.

In the meantime, combine egg yolks with one-quarter cup sugar in the top of the double boiler (but not over heat). Beat with rotary beater or portable electric mixer until very thick and fluffy; beat in rum.

Cook mixture over hot water in bottom of double boiler (water should not boil). Beat constantly; cook about ten minutes, until slightly thickened.

Remove from heat.

Cut up chocolate squares. Place chocolate in a small bowl; set bowl in a pan of hot, not boiling, water. Melt chocolate, stirring occasionally, over medium heat.

With wooden spoon, gradually beat melted chocolate into egg yolk mixture until well blended.

Then set top of double boiler in cold water to cool, beating with a wooden spoon, until very thick.

Now beat egg whites, with mixer at medium speed, until soft peaks form. Gradually beat in one-quarter cup sugar; beat until egg whites form stiff peaks when beater is raised.

Turn cooled chocolate mixture into egg whites. With wire whisk, fold in chocolate until blended. Turn into serving bowl or four small soufflé dishes.

Refrigerate until very well chilled—overnight preferably. Just before serving, decorate tops with mounds of whipped cream.

You will need:

15½ x 10½ x 1-inch
jelly roll pan
Waxed paper
Electric mixer with large
and small mixer bowls
Sifter or strainer
Rubber scraper
Wire whisk
Dish towel

4 egg whites
¾ cup sifted cake flour
1 teaspoon baking powder
¼ teaspoon salt
4 egg yolks
¾ cup fine granulated sugar
1 teaspoon vanilla extract
1 cup currant jelly

JELLY ROLL

Gâteau Roulé à la Confiture

(For 10)

Let egg whites warm to room temperature in large bowl of electric mixer—about one hour.

In the meantime, lightly grease the bottom of the jelly roll pan. Cut a sheet of waxed paper to fit bottom of the pan; fit paper into pan and grease lightly.

Preheat oven to 375°F. Sift cake flour, with baking powder and salt, through sifter on sheet of waxed paper.

In small bowl of electric mixer, beat egg yolks at high speed, until very thick and yellow. Gradually beat in sugar; continue beating until very thick.

With rubber scraper, gradually beat flour mixture into yolks only until flour mixture does not show any longer. Add vanilla. Wash beaters. At high speed, with clean beaters, beat egg whites until stiff peaks form. Using wire whisk, gently fold yolk mixture into egg whites, just until combined.

Turn into prepared jelly roll pan, spreading batter evenly.

Bake 12 to 15 minutes. To test cake for doneness: Gently press top with fingertip; if finger leaves an indentation, cake is not baked. Cake should spring back when pressed with fingertip. Do not overbake.

Meanwhile, onto a clean towel, sift confectioners' sugar in a 15 x 10-inch rectangle.

With sharp knife, loosen sides of cake from pan. Turn out cake onto sugar; gently peel off waxed paper. With knife, trim off crisp edges of cake.

Starting with the long edge, roll cake in towel; place, seam side down, on wire rack until cooled completely.

Gently unroll cake; remove towel. Spread cake with jelly (beaten with fork to spreading consistency). Reroll.

Place, seam side down, on serving plate; cover loosely with foil. Chill at least one hour.

To serve, lightly sift confectioners' sugar over top. Slice on diagonal with serrated knife.

VITAL DETAILS

Les Détails

"Much depends on dinner," Byron said some time ago. If this is true, then much depends on small details, for in the serving of a perfect meal, nothing is left to chance.

If you are a wise hostess, you will plan your meal in advance. You will prepare soups and stews, sauces and desserts well ahead of time, so that you are free to do other things before the meal. In addition, many of these dishes improve on standing. You need only to reheat and taste them for the final seasoning, then arrange them on platters and garnish attractively for serving.

The less important points, but vital, nevertheless, should be second nature to the clever hostess.

Remember that serving platters, dinner plates, and even the coffee cups should always be preheated, the salad plates and the white wine glasses prechilled.

Salad greens should be prepared and crisped ahead of time.

Cheeses (except cream cheese) should be taken from the refrigerator, long enough before serving, to warm to room temperature. Cheeses should be "ripe" when served so that they will have their characteristic flavor. For example, Camembert is at peak flavor when it is soft, not firm.

The last point the wise hostess should remember is that the coffee should be absolutely perfect, with a robust, hearty flavor and aroma, not overly strong or "overcooked" in flavor. Once the coffee is made, the coffee grounds should be removed. And when you keep coffee hot, remember that it should never be allowed to boil.

HOT CHOCOLATE
Chocolat
(For 6)

In the top of a double boiler, combine 2 squares of unsweetened chocolate, ¼ cup sugar, a dash of salt and ½ cup water. Place over hot water; cook until chocolate is melted. Stir in 4 cups of milk. Heat until thoroughly hot. Just before serving, beat with egg beater.

For an extra treat, float a marshmallow on top of each cup, or spoon on a mound of whipped cream.

DRIP COFFEE
Café

For each serving, use 1½ to 2 tablespoons (standard measure) of ground coffee and ¾ measuring cup boiling water. To obtain the very best flavor, grind the coffee beans just before brewing. Coffee which is not freshly ground loses its full flavor.

Put the coffee pot in a "bain-marie," that is, a pan of hot water, so that the coffee will not cool while it drips.

First, measure the desired amount of coffee (drip grind) into filter section of coffee pot. Add ¾ cup boiling water; let coffee steep five minutes to develop its aroma. Then, cup by cup, add the rest of the boiling water.

Coffee should always be served hot, and preferably in heated cups!

TEA
Thé

It's best to use a china, pottery or heat resistant glass tea pot. Make sure the pot is very clean!

Just before making tea, fill tea pot with boiling water; let it stand a few minutes to heat pot, then pour off the water.

Put tea leaves in the pot—use 1 to 1½ teaspoons (standard measure) tea for each cup of water. Pour on the desired amount of boiling water. Water should come fresh from the tap, brought to a good boil and poured over tea at once. Let steep 3 to 5 minutes—until tea reaches desired strength. Remember, however, that tea becomes bitter when steeped overly long.

Strain tea into another heated pot or into cups.

PINK LEMONADE

Limonade Rose

(For 4)

Squeeze 3 or 4 lemons to make enough juice to measure 1 cup. Pour juice into pitcher along with ¾ cup sugar syrup.* For a pretty pink color, add a little grenadine—about 2 tablespoons. Add 1½ cups ice water. Stir to mix well. Pour over ice cubes in tall glasses.

FRUITS OF "PARADISE" COCKTAIL

Cocktail Jus de Fruits "Paradise"
From the "Epi-Club" at Saint-Tropez

(For 6)

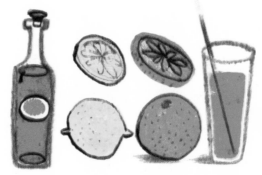

In a large pitcher, combine ⅓ cup lemon juice, 2 cups orange juice, ¾ cup sugar syrup*, 1 tablespoon grenadine, 1½ cups ice water, several lemon and orange slices. Mix well. Pour into glasses, filled with ice cubes. Garnish with orange or lemon slices and a maraschino cherry with stem.

ORANGEADE

Orangeade

(For 6)

Squeeze 4 oranges to make 1 cup of juice. Set juice aside.

Put leftover orange peels in a saucepan with 1 cup water and ¾ cup sugar. Bring to boiling point. Cover, reduce heat to low, and cook very slowly, about five minutes. Set aside to cool. Discard orange peels.

Add orange juice and 2 cups of water to syrup in saucepan. Mix well. Taste, and add some sugar if needed. Serve over ice in glasses.

* Sugar syrup: Combine ½ cup sugar and ½ cup water in a saucepan. Heat, stirring, just until sugar is dissolved. Let cool before using. Makes ¾ cup.

CLUB SANDWICH

Club-Sandwich
(For 1)

Spread two slices of white bread, on one side only, with soft butter or mayonnaise. On the buttered side of one slice, place a lettuce leaf (washed and crisped); cover with tomato slices, a slice of ham, a slice of chicken and an anchovy. Then top with another lettuce leaf and the second slice of bread, buttered side down. Spear with several cocktail picks to hold all firmly in place. Decorate picks with stuffed olives.

STUFFED BREAD

Pain-Bagnat
(For 2)

In a chopping bowl, chop together 1 stalk of celery, 1 pimiento, 3 green olives and 3 black olives (all pitted) and 3 Hard-Cooked Eggs, see page 30. Add ¼ cup mayonnaise, ½ teaspoon salt and dash of pepper; toss together lightly to mix well.

Slice across the top of a small loaf of French bread or a large hard roll. With a fork, scoop some of the bread out of the bottom half. Line the opening with crisp lettuce, then fill with the egg salad, mounding it up high. Keep refrigerated until serving time.

Nice for a day at the beach!

HERO SANDWICH

Sandwich-Repas
(For 1 or 2)

Split a small loaf of French bread in half lengthwise. Then spread each cut half with soft butter. Spread bottom half with mustard if you like.

Set top half of bread aside. Starting at one end of the bottom half of the bread, arrange several slices of ham, each rolled up, then several slices of salami, also in rolls, to completely cover the bottom half.

Top with a second layer of sliced Gruyère cheese and a third layer of sliced tomatoes or pimientos. Sprinkle with sliced green and black olives and cover with lettuce.

Complete by placing the top half of the bread over all. Bon appétit!

GLOSSARY OF COOKING TERMS

Lexique des Termes de Cuisine

ASPIC—Gelatine with a meat, vegetable or wine base. Used to mold other foods or as a garnish.

AU JUS—Natural juice. Used, for example, to refer to meat served in its own juice.

BLANCH—To remove the outer covering of fruits, vegetables or nuts by letting them stand in boiling water until the skin or shell comes off easily.

BOIL—To cook at the boiling point, that is, the surface of the liquid breaks into small waves.

BRAISE—To brown meat or vegetables in a small amount of hot fat and cook slowly, tightly covered. Additional liquid may or may not be added.

BROCHETTE—Small spit or skewer used for broiling meat cubes.

BROIL—To cook directly under a flame or heating unit or over an open fire or grill.

CARAMELIZE—To melt sugar slowly over very low heat until it becomes liquid, golden-brown, and has a caramel flavor.

CREAM—To beat shortening until smooth, creamy and light, using a wooden spoon or beater.

DICE—To cut food into small cubes, less than one-half inch in diameter.

FLAKE—To break or pull apart a food, such as fish, in which there are natural divisions. Food may be flaked by following these divisions, pulling at them gently with one or two forks or with the fingers.

FLAMBÉ—To add brandy or cognac to a food, and then ignite. The alcohol burns off, giving the food a distinctive flavor.

FOLD—To combine two ingredients. Beaten egg whites, for example, are folded very gently with wire whisk or rubber scraper, using an under-and-over motion, until thoroughly incorporated into another mixture.

FRY—(1) To cook in a small amount of fat on top of stove, also called "pan-fry." (2) To cook a food in a deep layer of hot fat, called "deep-frying."

GRATE—To shred particles of food by rubbing the food by hand against a grater. Particles vary from fine to coarse depending upon the size of the hole in the grater.

MARINATE—To soak food, meat or vegetables, in acid such as lemon juice or in wine or in an oil-acid mixture like French dressing. The marinade acts as a tenderizer and/or increases the flavor.

MELT—To heat solid food, like sugar or fat, until it liquefies.

PARE—To remove the thin outer covering of vegetables and fruits with a paring knife or parer.

PURÉE—To press soft fruits or vegetables through a sieve or food mill or to blend in an electric blender until pulpy.

SAUTÉ—To fry foods until golden and tender in a small amount of fat in skillet.

SIFT—To put flour through a sifter or sieve, then measure by spooning lightly into cup and leveling off excess.

SIMMER—To cook just below the boiling point adjusting the heat to maintain this stage. In simmering, the food cooks so slowly the surface moves only slightly and no bubbles appear.

SKEWER—To thread foods, such as meat, fish, poultry or vegetables, on a wooden or metal skewer, so that they hold their shape during broiling.

STEW—To cook foods very slowly, in just enough liquid to cover them. Always keep liquid below the boiling point.

When measuring ingredients, it is important to always use the standard measuring equipment described on page 6.

A FINAL WORD

En Sortant de la Cuisine

When you're finished in the kitchen, check to be sure you've turned off the gas or electricity, washed all the dishes and utensils you've used, and hung up the dish towels to dry.

We're certain you will be using this book over and over again, and we hope that you'll have many pleasant hours in the kitchen. *Bon appétit!*